Andy Croft has written or edited over 80 books – poetry, fiction, biography and non-fiction. He has worked as a writer-in-residence in several prisons, including HMPs Holme House, Moorland and Lindholme. He is the author of *Forty-six Quid and a Bag of Dirty Washing*, published by Diffusion in 2014.

About Diffusion books

Diffusion publishes books for adults who are emerging readers. There are two series:

 Books in the Diamond series are ideally suited to those who are relatively new to reading or who have not practised their reading skills for some time (approximately Entry Level 2 to 3 in adult literacy levels).

 Books in the Star series are for those who are ready for the next step. They will help to build confidence and inspire readers to tackle longer books (approximately Entry Level 3 to Level 1 in adult literacy levels).

Other books available in the Star series are

Not Such a Bargain by Toby Forward

Barcelona Away by Tom Palmer

Forty-six Quid and a Bag of Dirty Washing by Andy Croft

One Shot by Lena Semaan

BARE FREEDOM

ANDY CROFT

diffusion

First published in Great Britain in 2016

Diffusion
an imprint of
SPCK
36 Causton Street
London SW1P 4ST
www.spck.org.uk

ISBN 978-1-908713-03-2

Typeset by Graphicraft Limited, Hong Kong
First printed in Great Britain by Ashford Colour Press
Subsequently digitally reprinted in Great Britain

Produced on paper from sustainable forests

*In memory of Carl Jacques
(1977–2015).*

Thanks again to Insy.

*This book is for anyone trying to walk
a straight line in a crooked world.*

Freedom means warmth and protection against harsh exposure to the elements. It means food, not garbage. It means truth, harmony, and the social relations that spring from these. It means the best medical attention whenever it's needed. It means employment that is reasonable, that coincides with the individual necessities and feelings.

George Jackson, *Blood in My Eye* (1971)

Contents

1

Love your probation officer

———••◆•◆••———

Barry gave his name to the woman behind the glass. She nodded at him and asked him to wait. He sat down on one of the comfy chairs by the window and smiled up at the CCTV camera.

He was early, as usual. These days Barry was always early. He knew that he could not afford to be late for a meeting with his probation officer. So he always arrived far too soon.

Every Tuesday for the past month Barry had been coming here to meet with his probation officer, or 'offender manager' as he liked to call himself. Barry was never really sure what the point of these meetings was supposed to be. They had discussed his licence conditions at the first meeting. But since then they seemed to spend most of the time talking about Barry's hopes and his feelings. The probation officer kept saying, 'Yes, Barry, but how do you *feel*?'

The probation officer seemed friendly. He told Barry to call him Colin.

Yet Barry knew that this man could have him recalled to prison in a heartbeat. Barry tried to play along. But there was no way he was going to start talking about the things that really mattered with a probation officer.

On the other side of the glass, people were busy typing on their computers. Some were wearing headsets and seemed to be talking to themselves. Behind the main desk there was a huge pot plant and a fish tank. On the far wall was a poster that said: 'Keep Calm and Love Your Probation Officer'.

In the tank a large blue fish was swimming round and round, as though it was looking for something. He could see why some lads called Seg the 'fish tank'. This poor old fish was in solitary 24/7. There was nowhere it could hide from the gaze of anyone watching. Round and round and round it went. No matter how far or how fast it swam, the fish always ended up back where it started. So much effort without ever getting anywhere, thought Barry. He knew how the fish felt.

The water-cooler burped as he poured himself a plastic cup of cold water. The woman behind the glass was talking on the telephone. As she did so, she was trying to scratch her back between her shoulders with a pencil. Behind her the office was full of filing cabinets and computers, reports and assessments. All this was needed to keep tabs on people like Barry.

He tried to imagine the world these people lived in – their holiday rotas, pension plans and leaving parties. Did the guy with the beard fancy that young black woman sitting at the desk next to him? Was that fat bloke stuffing his face with crisps worried about his weight? Did any of them ever try to imagine the lives of the people who passed through this office? Or were people like Barry just numbers to them?

Back in the tank, the fish was still swimming round and round. Whatever it was looking for, Barry felt certain the fish was not going to find it. A fish only has three seconds of memory. Then everything starts again. A new beginning, a fresh start, a clean slate, a new leaf – all the things they like to talk about in this place. The only problem was that the slate was never completely wiped clean here. There was always a file somewhere, a piece of paper or a digital memory. The past followed you around like a dog. No matter how fast you ran, your record was always there, sniffing at your heels, reminding you of your mistakes.

Eventually Barry was buzzed through the glass doors. Colin was waiting for him. His glasses hung round his neck in the usual tangle of security passes, car-park tokens and name badges. Barry smiled to himself as he pictured the headline in the local newspaper: 'Probation Officer Strangles Himself with Own Security Pass'.

He followed Colin into a small office at the end of the corridor. It was bare except for a table and two chairs, a flip-chart and another pot plant. There were bars on the frosted windows. Someone had written 'What is freedom?' in red pen on the flip-chart. Good question, thought Barry.

Colin looked up from the file in front of him and took his glasses off. 'Well, Barry,' he said with a grin, 'I think it's payback time.'

What do you think?

Why is Barry always so early?

Why does Barry think he knows how the fish feels?

Do you think it is ever possible to wipe the slate clean?

2

Little Chris

———•◦•———

Outside the probation office, Barry stopped to roll a tab.

Colin had talked to him about the Community Payback programme. Barry felt his heart sink. He had done this stuff once before, when it was called Community Service. He had wandered around the town in a bright orange jacket, scraping chewing-gum off the pavements. Barry did not mind doing things that were really useful. But he had once spent the best part of a week trying to clean some graffiti off the walls of the railway station underpass. The graffiti had been really pretty, unlike the underpass.

Suddenly he heard a shout. 'Baz!'

Only one person ever called him that. Little Chris. And here he was, wearing his drugs-dealer shades and bling. He was with two of his minders. Barry knew what this was about.

Barry said to him, 'Chris. All right? No worries, Chris. I've told you. You'll get your money. I just need some time to get sorted.'

A few years ago Barry was meant to deliver some phet for Little Chris to a flat on the Meadows estate. He had stopped at an off-licence to ask for directions. When he came back outside, the car had gone. So had the drugs. Of course, Chris had blamed him. Going to jail usually meant that your debts were cancelled. But Chris was not like that. Ever since Barry had got out of prison Chris had been hassling him for the money. And Chris did not make threats. He just made demands.

Chris replied, 'What makes you think I'm here to talk about money, Baz? We go back a long way, you and me.'

Exactly, thought Barry.

'But now you mention it,' Chris continued, 'how much was it? I've forgotten. How much of my money did you lose? How much do you still owe me?'

Barry sighed. 'You know. Eight hundred quid. And it wasn't my fault.'

Little Chris whistled. 'That's a lot of dosh, mate. But I tell you what, I'll forget the interest. For old times' sake.' He pushed his face towards Barry's and said, 'You've got a month. Then you're working for me.' Chris turned to go, but then added, 'Oh, I almost forgot. Abi sends her love.' He blew Barry a kiss and disappeared into the crowded street.

Barry took several deep breaths and tried to calm his rising anger. As he lit up, he realized that he was shaking.

In prison, most lads had photos of a girlfriend on their pad walls. Some had photos of their children. But Barry did not have a girlfriend. And he did not have any kids. The only picture on his cell wall had been a photo of him and Abi. It had been taken on a trip to the zoo when they were kids. Since the death of their nan, Abi was the only family he had left. On his last sentence, Abi had got involved with Little Chris. Somehow Barry had to try to get her away from him.

But he also had to pay Little Chris the money.

If Barry agreed to work for Little Chris his debts would be cleared, and he might be able to look out for Abi.

On the other hand, he knew that working for Little Chris was the quickest way of ending up back inside.

Barry finished his tab and bought a packet of crisps at the newsagent's on the corner. There was a black dog by the railings. It was a thin-looking greyhound in a bad way. Its ears had been cut off. Some people lost interest in a greyhound the minute it stopped winning races. And you can't trace a dog with no ears. This one was lucky it had not been buried alive. Barry shook his head at the thought of such cruelty.

He bent down to stroke the dog. As he raised his hand the dog flinched. 'It's OK,' said Barry, 'I'm not going to hurt you.'

Judging by the thin ribs showing through its skin, the dog had not been fed in a while. Barry offered the dog some crisps. The dog looked at Barry for a moment, as if unsure whether or not to trust him. Then it started to nibble the crisps.

'Here, you can finish them,' said Barry, tipping the crisps out onto the pavement. 'Looks like you're even hungrier than me.' He left the dog wolfing down the last of the crisps.

For the next couple of hours Barry walked round the town centre, trying to work out what to do about Little Chris. Outside the leisure centre he caught sight of his reflection in the mirrored windows. He badly needed a shave and a haircut. If he was not careful he was going to end up a mad loner talking to his own reflection. Eventually he sat down on one of the benches outside the central library and rolled another tab. He was almost out of burn.

He felt something brush against his leg. It was the dog, underneath the bench, looking up at him expectantly. 'Go on, boy!' said Barry. 'Go home. I haven't got any more crisps. Go on! Clear off.' The dog refused to budge. Barry pretended to throw a stick for the dog to chase. Still the dog would not move. Barry went and sat on a different bench. The dog followed him.

The dog was still trotting beside him when Barry reached the gate of the bail hostel. 'Sorry, lad,' said Barry, bending down to stroke the greyhound. 'You can't come in here.'

The dog looked up at him with its big greyhound eyes.

'Anyway, you wouldn't like it. Take it from me.'

What do you think?

What does Barry think about the Community Payback programme?

Why doesn't Barry want to work for Little Chris?

Why do you think the greyhound follows Barry?

3

It's a free country

Barry sat down at the kitchen table in the bail hostel. His key-worker, Barbara, said, 'I'm just putting the kettle on, Barry. How do you like your tea?'

Barry replied, 'Black no sugar, please, Barbara.'

Barry looked at the poster on the wall above him. It said, 'No alcohol. No smoking. No non-prescription drugs.' Barry half expected the list to say, 'No running. No jumping. No talking. No breathing.' The whole system was based on telling you what you could not do.

Barbara was a big woman in her forties, with big hair and dangly earrings. She looked as if she ate too much cake. She put two cups of tea down on the table and pulled out a pile of forms. As usual, she had put both milk and sugar in Barry's tea.

Barbara sat down and said, 'Nothing to worry about, Barry. Just routine. You know the score by now. We need you to take another VDT.'

Barry never knew why they were called 'voluntary' drugs tests, because there was nothing voluntary about them. He sighed. He had been clean for the past two years. He had Gaz, his old pad-mate, to thank for that. Not that it had been easy. He knew plenty of lads who were clean when they started their sentences but when they left a couple of years later they were sprouting needles.

Barry was not worried about failing the piss-test. But he hated being asked. It was like asking small boys to turn out their pockets. It always made him feel guilty. Also, he had heard quite a few stories about dodgy test results.

But, of course, he did not dare say anything. If he tried to protest it would look like he had something to hide. It did not take much to be recalled – a missed appointment, a misunderstanding, an argument. He knew a lad once who was recalled from a bail hostel just because he had forgotten to empty the waste-bin in his room. Another ended up back inside just because his key-worker suspected he was *thinking* of doing something. How do you defend yourself against that? Barry did not fancy going back to the local Cat B. He had left behind some bad memories there.

There were so many rules in a bail hostel. There were curfews, morning meetings, action plans, supervision plans, risk assessments, purposeful activity, progress reviews and drugs tests. Barry thought they were like tripwires, trapdoors and landmines. One false step and you were gone.

Back in his room, Barry sat on the edge of the bed and rolled a tab. In the cemetery behind the hostel a woman and two small children were feeding bread to the pigeons. The youngest child kept trying to eat the bread. A man in yellow Lycra cycled down the path towards the park.

Barry leaned out of the window and sparked up. In the large house across the road there was a young woman sitting at the bedroom window. She was staring into nothing. She had short blonde hair that was nicely cut. She had a pretty face. Barry guessed that she was probably about seventeen. Barry was only twenty-four, but he felt a lot older. Everything about the girl seemed to represent the life of freedom that Barry wanted. She had smart hair and a big house, with new 4x4s parked outside. Barry envied her youth and freedom. Like the people down there on the grass, she was free to go anywhere, to do anything she wanted.

Barry suddenly felt lonely. He tried to imagine the life of the girl, and the lives of the other people in the big house. Did she have a job? Did she have a boyfriend? Barry decided that she was a student, living at home with her wealthy parents. There was something spoilt and sulky about her expression, as though she was always wishing she was somewhere else. He knew that a girl like this would never understand how hard his life had been, or how few choices he had ever really had.

He was supposed to be a free man now, wasn't he? Yet his life was squeezed by the demands of probation, the benefit office, the Jobcentre, the bail hostel and Little Chris. All he wanted to do was to start again. He wanted to find Abi, to get a job and rent a flat.

Barry wondered why it all felt so difficult. It was meant to be a free country, but it didn't feel like one.

He finished his tab. As he shut the window the girl looked up and saw him. He smiled and waved.

She blanked him.

What do you think?

Why does Barbara put milk and sugar in Barry's tea?

Why does Barry resent being asked to take a VDT?

Do you think it is a free country?

4

Independence

The next morning, the dog was waiting for him at the end of the drive.

'You're not getting a bag of crisps every day, you know,' said Barry, patting the greyhound. The dog did not seem to mind. He followed Barry all the way to the Jobcentre.

The Jobcentre was in a shiny new building but the place was as depressing as the old offices on Market Street. Although everything was now computerized, it was still the same nightmare. The busy staff seemed even more unhelpful than he remembered.

The system had changed a lot since Barry last tried to sign on. For one thing, there were unsmiling security guards on the door. They looked like bouncers outside a nightclub.

Jobseeker's Allowance was being replaced by a means-tested system called Universal Credit. You could only apply for this online. Barry did not own a computer so, on his first visit, he had to queue to use one of the ones available at the Jobcentre. When he finally got his turn he had to answer lots of questions, like, 'What was your annual income last year from investment and property?' and 'How much do you pay into a private pension scheme?'

Eventually the computer screen showed that Barry could get £73.34 a week. This did not seem a lot of money. But the computer explained that it was an increase of 24p on what he would have got under the old system! At least it would help him to get back on his feet until he found a job. Things were looking up at last, thought Barry.

But then the problems started. First, it turned out that the bail hostel would take some of this money before Barry even saw it. This was to pay for his rent, breakfast, bedding and towels.

'How much?' Barry asked one of the Jobcentre Plus advisors.

'It could be anything up to forty-four pounds a week,' she replied.

'What?' Barry exclaimed. 'You mean I've got to live on less than thirty quid a week?'

'Just until you find a job.'

'But how long is that going to take?' asked Barry. 'I've still got to live till then, haven't I?'

The advisor looked across the room at one of the security gorillas and said, 'Please don't raise your voice like that, sir. We have a strict policy of zero-tolerance of aggression towards staff.'

'I'm sorry,' said Barry. 'I didn't mean to shout. It's just that . . .'

The woman cut him off. 'Remember that the new system is simply designed to help you become more independent . . .'

Next, it turned out that Barry could not claim Universal Credit without a National Insurance number. He had no idea if he had ever had one of these. The advisor explained that he could apply for one. 'It's very easy,' she assured him. 'All you need is a passport.'

Barry tried to explain that he had never had a passport.

She sighed, and asked, 'How about a current driving licence?'

His provisional driving licence had run out years ago.

'Well, do you have a birth certificate?' asked the exasperated advisor.

Barry was tempted to say that he could prove that he had been born, but he thought she would not get the joke. In the end she told him that he would have to attend an 'Evidence of Identity' interview so that he could apply for a National Insurance number.

Next, the advisor told Barry that they needed his bank account details.

'But I haven't got a bank account,' he explained. 'I've got no money. I'm completely broke. That's why I'm here.' This was ridiculous. Barry was beginning to lose his patience. 'What would I want with a bank account? If I had one I wouldn't be trying to sign on, would I?'

The advisor looked at Barry as though he was stupid. 'You have to open a bank account so we can pay you your Universal Credit,' she explained. 'Anyway, it's very easy. All you need is—'

'Don't tell me,' said Barry. 'Let me guess – a passport or a driving licence?'

'Anyway, don't worry,' said the advisor. 'There's no rush to open a bank account. You won't receive your first payment for a while yet.'

'How do you mean?' asked Barry.

She explained that the money would be paid into his bank account monthly, not every week. 'This is to help you learn to manage your money better,' she explained. 'Budgeting and so on.'

Barry started to ask, 'But how can I budget when I haven't got any money?'

But she ignored him. 'The first payment will be paid into your new account one calendar month and seven days after you submit your claim.'

Barry stared at the woman in disbelief. 'You're joking? That's five weeks! *Five weeks!* How am I supposed to live until then?' He realized he was shouting again. One of the gorillas was watching him. He took a deep breath and sat down. The last thing he needed was to be in trouble before he had even made a claim.

'Sorry,' he said. 'It's just— I mean—' He took another deep breath. 'Can I apply for a loan? I mean, just until I get this money. Till I get sorted. Just till I get a job.'

The woman smiled. 'Of course. Benefit claimants are entitled to apply for an emergency "budgeting loan" of up to three hundred and forty-eight pounds.'

'Great,' said Barry, with relief. 'So how do I apply for one of them?'

'Unfortunately, you have to be on income-related benefit for at least twenty-six weeks before you can apply,' she explained.

Barry was speechless with frustration. Did this woman have any idea what this meant? Did she care? How did she expect him to live for the next five weeks?

The woman smiled sweetly at Barry, as though reading his thoughts. 'You can always try a food bank . . .'

What do you think?

Why does Barry describe the Jobcentre as a nightmare?

Why do you think it is so difficult to claim benefit these days?

How is Barry expected to live until he receives his first Universal Credit payment?

5

Jackson

———•◦•———

Barry did not usually believe in conspiracy theories. Prison was full of lads obsessed with crazy stories about the Apollo moon landings or 9/11. But it felt like the system was designed to send you back to prison as quickly as possible. Unless you had a family waiting for you when you got out, you stood little chance of staying out. The benefit system was certainly not there for Barry's benefit. Staying out of prison was not a question of 'being good' or 'trying'. It was about not letting the system trip you up. But how could you do that when they deliberately tied your feet together with red tape?

Gaz, his old cellmate, used to say, 'It's all about feeding the machine. Some people make a big profit out of the prison system. Just imagine what would happen to those profits if the prisons were empty.'

This was one of Gaz's favourite subjects. He said that it was not by chance that the prison population in the UK had doubled in the past twenty years, just as more and more prisons and prison services were being run by companies trying to make a profit. Apparently the government was planning to privatize probation next.

'They need people like us,' Gaz used to say. 'The poor, the working class, the hopeless, the unlucky – they need us to fill their prisons. And to boost the profits of the big companies who run them. Every year the crime figures go down, and all the time they are building more and more prisons. They may talk a lot about rehabilitation, but really they want lots of people in prison because it means more money for them. The system's worst nightmare is actually an empty prison cell.'

By now, Barry was completely skint. It seemed that not many things in a free society were actually free. His £46 discharge grant had gone by the end of the second week. His old mate Craig had lent him £20, but Barry knew he could not live for ever on hand-outs. Anyway, he needed to pay that back. He would have to fill up for the day on toast and tea at breakfast in the hostel. But he badly needed some new clothes. For one thing, he only had two pairs of underpants. For another, the sole of one of his trainers was starting to flap.

Outside the Jobcentre the dog with no ears was waiting for him again. 'Hello, boy,' said Barry, crouching down to hug the old greyhound. He had become strangely attached to this dog. He and the dog were both outsiders, unwanted and a bit battered. No one knew where the dog came from and no one cared. Barry knew how it felt. Anyway, everyone needed at least one friendly face in an unfriendly world.

'Look, mate, if you are going to follow me around all day, I reckon we need to be properly introduced,' said Barry, taking off his baseball cap. 'I'm Barry. Pleased to meet you.' He put his cap back on. 'And you – you need a name.' He thought for a minute. 'Jackson. From now on I'm going to call you Jackson. After a hero of mine. I'll tell you all about him one day.'

Gaz had told Barry all about George Jackson. Jackson was an African American, sentenced to life imprisonment in San Quentin prison, California, for robbing $70 from a garage when he was eighteen. In prison he started reading and writing, and he wrote a couple of books. He was shot in mysterious circumstances in the prison when he was just thirty years old.

One night Gaz had copied out some of Jackson's words from one of his books and stuck them on the wall above the toilet in their shared pad:

It is not important to me how long I live, I think only of how I live, how well, how nobly . . . if we are to be men again we must stop working for nothing, competing against each other for the little they allow us to possess, stop selling our women or allowing them to be used and handled against their will.

Just before Barry got out, Gaz had given him the book. That way, Gaz said, Barry would not forget Jackson's words.

What do you think?

What would happen if all the prisons were empty? Can you imagine what it would be like?

Why does Barry decide to name the dog after George Jackson?

What do you think George Jackson meant by 'living nobly'?

6

Criminal

———◆•◆———

Every time Barry stepped through the doors of the Jobcentre he felt like he was in a science-fiction nightmare. Or as if he was back inside. Sometimes it seemed that there were more security staff in the place than claimants. They stared at him as he went through the doors. Barry half expected one of them to ask him for his number.

The way they looked at him made Barry feel like he had committed a crime. Of course, he *had* committed a crime – plenty of them. But he had done his time; he had paid the price. He was meant to be a free man. Free to find a job. Free to start again. And yet everything seemed designed to make him feel guilty for being here at all.

Anyone applying for Universal Credit had to sign a 'claimant commitment'. Barry's commitment said he had to spend thirty-five hours a week looking for work online. As he did not have a computer, he had to be at the Jobcentre five days a week, from 9 a.m. to 5 p.m., so that he could go online. Barry had no money for bus fares, so he walked the two miles to the Jobcentre and back every day in his old trainers. The sole of his other trainer was also beginning to flap.

Once Barry had set up an account at the Jobcentre, he had to create a profile and write a CV. But he did not know how to describe himself without sounding vague or dishonest. 'I am a keen, polite, hard-working and reliable person.' Too strong. 'I am friendly and flexible.' Sounds weird. 'I am a desperate ex-con with no useful experience who will do anything to get a job.' Too honest.

And what should he put under 'achievements'? One rusty GCSE in maths? Houseblock 1 table-tennis champion? Being clean for two years? Missing his nan's funeral on his last sentence?

He also had to list his 'spare-time activities'. What spare time? Barry used to like reading and playing chess with Gaz. But since getting out, his entire week was taken up with meetings at the bail hostel, with probation and at the Jobcentre. Yesterday, Barbara at the bail hostel told him that they expected him to keep a weekly diary. When was he going to find time to do that?

If you did not like the sound of the first job they offered you, they stopped your benefit for three months. If you said no to two jobs there would be no benefit for six months. Three refusals, and you lost any benefits for three years. But there were no jobs. Or at least there were no jobs for Barry. He had expected to be offered some back-breaking job on a zero-hours contract. But it seemed that even those jobs were out of Barry's reach.

Everywhere there were signs warning him what would happen if he got paid for work while claiming benefit. But after four weeks of trying, he still had not managed to do either.

Because there was always a wait to use the computers in the Jobcentre, Barry sometimes used the computers in the central library. The Jobcentre staff could still access his account to check how many jobs he was applying for each week.

After a while Barry got to know some of the other regulars at the Jobcentre. At midday they usually met outside for a sandwich and a cup of tea from the shop across the road. Jackson was always waiting for them by the railings, happy to accept the crusts they gave him.

They often swapped stories about the rudeness of the Jobcentre advisors and the cruelty of the system.

'Did you hear about that old bloke whose benefit was stopped for a month because he was seen selling poppies for Remembrance Sunday?' An unemployed librarian called Liz usually took the lead in these conversations. She was full of stories of how people had had their benefit stopped, or been 'sanctioned', as it was officially called.

'Why?' asked Barry.

Liz explained. 'Because he wasn't "actively seeking work", according to the Jobcentre.'

'That's ridiculous!' said Hanif, one of the other regulars.

'Well,' Liz said, 'that's the Department of Work and Pensions for you.'

They all shook their heads and watched Jackson help himself to the remains of their sandwiches.

'Look at your dog, Barry,' said Liz.

'He's not my dog,' said Barry. 'But I'm looking. What about him?'

Liz said, 'You see how happy he is to eat the bits of sandwich that Hanif doesn't want? Well that's us.'

'How do you mean?' said Hanif.

Liz answered, 'He's happy with the scraps.'

'He's certainly enjoying Hanif's chicken sarnie,' said Barry.

'I mean, look at us,' Liz continued. 'Happy with the crusts from the rich man's table. Just think how grateful we all are that we haven't been sanctioned yet.'

'Speak for yourself,' said Hanif. 'They stopped my benefit once because I had a job interview, which meant that I was late for my appointment at the Jobcentre.'

'Did you get the job?' asked Barry.

'Course not,' said Hanif.

'That's because there are no jobs,' said Liz. 'Not real ones. And it doesn't matter how many jobs we apply for, we can still get sanctioned. Last year *over a million people* had their benefit stopped. There was a bloke on the news last week who applied for hundreds of jobs, but they still stopped his benefit.'

'Why?' asked Barry.

Liz said, 'Because he didn't get enough replies.'

'You're joking!' said Hanif.

'Honest,' said Liz. 'Wasn't exactly his fault, was it? They say they want us to work, but they know that there are no jobs. They don't want us to be unemployed. They don't want us to claim benefit. They don't want us to beg on the streets. So what are we supposed to do? Jump in the sea?'

It seemed to Barry that there was only one place he was going to end up.

And that was back inside.

What do you think?

Why does Barry feel that he is back inside when he goes to the Jobcentre?

How would you describe yourself on a job application?

What do you think society expects Barry to do?

7

Hungry

———⋅•◆•⋅———

The shop was half-full. Perfect. If there were too many customers, he would not be able to run out if he was caught. But an empty shop was no good either. Barry had chosen this shop with care. The big supermarkets had security staff and cameras everywhere. And they *always* called the police. But small family businesses like this did not usually want to involve the police.

This shop was not too big, not too small, but just right, as Goldilocks might say. Not that Barry was looking for porridge. He knew that he would go straight back to jail if he was caught. But he told himself that the law of hunger outweighed the law of the land. Everyone had a right to eat, didn't they?

There were two people working in the shop. Barry guessed that they were father and son. The older man behind the till had a long, dark beard. The younger man was wearing a Liverpool shirt. Two teenagers came in. They were laughing loudly and pushing each other about. The man behind the till watched them anxiously as they moved down the shop. Then he went back to serving the customers waiting in the queue that was blocking one of the aisles. The man in the Liverpool shirt went out to the back of the shop.

The teenagers stopped at the fridge next to Barry, giggling nervously. Some other kids outside started banging on the shop window. Some of the older customers in the queue at the till looked disgusted at their behaviour. Barry knew what was coming next. One of the teenagers looked over his shoulder. He saw Barry watching him and winked. The other picked up a bottle of vodka and slipped it inside his coat. They turned to run out of the shop. But the man in the Liverpool shirt was blocking their path. He had a baseball bat in his hands.

Barry took a deep breath and walked past them to the door. He could hear a lot of shouting behind him. Jackson was waiting for him outside the shop. Barry kept on walking. He did not stop until he reached the park. He sat down on a bench and looked around. The only other person on the benches was a middle-aged woman feeding bread to the pigeons. Every now and again a seagull swooped down to nick the bread.

The pigeons were either too fat or too good-natured to put up a fight.

Eventually the woman got up and left. Barry emptied his pockets onto the bench beside him. Two tins of dog food. Jackson jumped onto the bench in excitement.

It was only then that Barry realized he did not have a tin-opener.

What do you think?

Do you think that everyone has a right to eat?

Why do you think Barry did not stop the teenagers stealing the bottle of vodka?

Can stealing ever be right?

8

Nightmare

———•◆•———

Barry woke up with a start. For a heartbeat he was not sure where he was. Then he saw the mustard green walls of his room in the bail hostel.

In the dream he had been back inside. And like all dreams, it had seemed real. More real than the bail hostel sometimes did. As usual he had found himself back on the 3s on Houseblock 5. Two screws were spinning his pad. For some reason one of them was wearing a Liverpool top. Gaz was there. So was Jackson – although no one seemed to think that this was a problem. Barry had no idea what they were looking for. Eventually one of the screws pulled something out of his mattress. 'Got it!' he shouted in triumph. It was a tin-opener. Barry started to protest. 'But I haven't got a tin-opener . . .' Then he had woken up.

Ever since getting out, Barry had been haunted by dreams of prison. The story-lines of these dreams were not always the same but they were always set in the same place: the pad he had shared with Gaz on Houseblock 5. You can take a man out of jail, but it takes a long time to take the jail out of a man. Some mornings Barry woke with the smell of the place in his nostrils. But he also woke with a strange sense of loss.

That was the weird part. These dreams were not really what you would call nightmares. Although part of Barry was always glad to escape from these dreams, another part of him wanted to stay asleep. He did not understand it. All the time he was inside he had dreamed of getting out. And now here he was dreaming of being back inside. It made no sense.

Inside and out. Outside and in. It was all very confusing. Maybe he had become too used to living in the system, perhaps he had become too used to prison life. Lots of lads talked about how difficult it was to adjust to living on the Out. It took time. He knew that. In jail you knew where you were. There were rules for this, rules for that. You couldn't take a piss without asking permission. Every day had a set pattern.

If you are down the gym it must be Tuesday. If you are in the library it's Thursday. If it's Friday, then it's Canteen. If it's chips for tea, it could be any day of the week.

Things were less fixed on the Out. Less reliable. Mates came and went. So did girlfriends. But there were still plenty of rules and regulations. In some ways there seemed to be more rules now than there had been in prison. Most screws let you get on with doing your time, just as long as you don't take the piss. But on the Out, Barry felt that he was always walking on thin ice.

Another word for all this, of course, was loneliness. Not for the first time, Barry realized how much he missed the lads on Houseblock 5. Especially Mo, Jonesey and Carl. And above all Gaz. Without them his last sentence would have felt even longer. Without Gaz he would still be the same idiot he was when he went in. Barry smiled when he thought about the mates he had left behind. Beating Jonesey at table tennis. Gaz shouting at the television in their pad. Mo trying to do press-ups.

They were the nearest to brothers he was ever going to have. They were his family. And he did not know when he was going to see them again.

'We're not just brothers, we're a *nation*,' Gaz used to argue. 'Do you know how many people are locked up on this little planet of ours?' he once asked Barry. 'I'll tell you – *nine million.* That's bigger than the population of London. There are more of us in here than the entire populations of Switzerland or Israel. We may speak different languages. We may have different-coloured skin. But our differences are nothing compared to what we've got in common.'

For some reason, friendships made inside were different. In prison you shared everything you had – burn and biscuits, letters and jokes, problems and grief. When you have nothing, you can share everything; it is only the people who have everything who have nothing to share.

Barry was now a free man. In theory he was free to do anything he wanted. 'Bare freedom,' as some of the lads would say. And yet somehow he felt less free than he had ever felt inside.

He had nothing, and he had no one to share it with. Nightmare.

That night Barry noticed that there was a different girl at the window of the house behind the hostel. He waved, but she did not seem to see him.

What do you think?

Why do you think Barry feels homesick for jail?

In what way are friendships made inside 'different'?

What do you think people in prison have in common?

9

Benefit fraud

———◆•◆———

'What's this?' demanded Craig.

'It's a dog,' said Barry, climbing into Craig's old van. 'What does it look like? A giraffe?'

Craig took another look at Jackson, and asked, 'What's happened to its ears?'

'He hasn't got any.'

'What? You mean he's deaf?'

Barry ignored this. So did Jackson.

Craig asked again, 'What happened to them?'

Barry sighed. 'His previous owner cut the ears off. That's what happened to them.'

'What?' said Craig.

'To remove the identity tattoos. So no one could trace the owner when the dog stopped racing,' explained Barry. 'It's called cruelty to animals.'

'All right, keep your hair on,' said Craig. 'I'm just saying I don't want any dog hairs on the seats. OK?'

Jackson and Barry looked round at the filthy state of the van.

Barry was helping Craig clear out an old house on the bypass. The old lady who had lived there had died, and her family wanted to sell it. Twenty pounds for a Saturday's work was not great. For one thing, it was a long way below the minimum wage. But at the moment, no one was offering Barry even that. Anyway, it was money in his pocket. At the same time, Barry knew that he would be recalled if he was caught working while signing on. Not that he had received any benefit yet. But he had to be careful. He did not want to give anyone a reason to phone the National Benefit Fraud Hotline.

It took Barry and Craig several hours to clear the house. The owner had been a bit of a hoarder. There were cupboards full of newspapers, jam-jars, bottles and empty tins. The attic was crammed with ancient suitcases and old clothes. The piano in the front room took some shifting. They had to drive to three different council waste-depots in order to avoid paying house-clearance charges. And it was hard work. By midday they were both covered in sweat and dust.

'Makes you think, doesn't it?' said Barry, when they had finished heaving the piano into the van.

'What?' said Craig.

'I mean, it makes you think about death. And life.'

'What?' said Craig again.

'This old lady. She must have lived in this house a long time. Maybe all her life, I don't know. And now it's all gone. All her stuff. And all her memories. There's nothing left to show that she was ever here.'

Craig shrugged. 'You haven't seen the back bedroom yet, Barry – it's full of books!'

'It's like Jackson here,' Barry continued. 'One minute he's chasing an electric hare round a track, winning money and eating like a king. Next minute someone cuts off his ears.'

'I don't think anyone cut off the old lady's ears,' laughed Craig.

Barry gave up. He was not sure what he was trying to say anyway.

There were hundreds of books in the back bedroom, some on shelves, some in tea-chests and some balanced in dusty piles.

'What are we going to do with all these?' Barry asked as he began putting the books in black bin-liners.

'Landfill,' said Craig. 'Why?'

'Can I see if there are any good ones?'

'Don't tell me you know how to read, Barry! Help yourself – but I don't think you'll find many "True Crime" books here.'

Barry looked through the books. They were mostly historical novels and romances. He fished out a book about chess and another about the stars.

'I need to get Jackson's ears sorted,' Barry said. 'I was hoping there might be a book here about looking after dogs.'

'Barry – you are just out of jail, you're unemployed, skint and living in a bail hostel. How are you going to be able to afford to take that dog to a vet? Have you any idea how much they charge these days? If you're going to get a dog, at least get one that looks like a dog.' Craig pointed at Jackson. 'This one looks like a mutant. Jackson the Alien Dog. You need to get rid of him, Barry.'

Jackson ignored this. So did Barry. Someone had tried to get rid of Jackson once before. It was not going to happen again. Not if Barry could help it. The feelings he had for this dog did not make sense.

But meeting Jackson was the only good thing that had happened to him since getting out. How sad was that?

What do you think?

Why did Barry risk losing his benefit by working for Craig? Was he right to do so?

What do you think Barry was trying to say about the old lady?

Why is Barry so attached to the dog?

10

The future is orange

The minibus stopped outside the cemetery.
There were four of them, plus the supervisor.

In their bright yellow work boots and bright
orange jackets they looked like Lego men. Except
that Lego figures did not usually have 'Community
Payback' written on their backs. Of course, it was
supposed to be embarrassing. The whole thing
was meant to shame them in public. Barry
supposed that it was better than being put in
the stocks. And at least it would get him out
of the Jobcentre for a few days.

The supervisor began by making a little speech
about the aims of the Community Payback
scheme. He reminded them that it was intended
to rehabilitate as well as to punish, and that they
might learn skills that would help them find a
job. Barry looked down at the litter-picker and
the pile of bin-bags at his feet.

The cemetery was badly overgrown in places.

Local authority spending cuts meant that the grass had not been mown for several months. The paths needed weeding and the litter needed collecting. Barry's job was to pick up all the crisp bags, broken bottles, empty cans and plastic bags before one of the other lads attacked the grass with a strimmer.

It was hot and difficult work. In some places the grass was too long and thick for the litter-picker to be of any use. Barry decided it was easier to get down on his knees and gather the rubbish by hand. By midday he had found a dead bird, a couple of syringes, several disposable nappies and a dozen used condoms. Barry also had the impression that most of the dogs in the area used the cemetery for a toilet. At least he was wearing gloves.

At midday they sat on one of the benches to eat. The other lads had brought sandwiches. Barry made a crisp sandwich with some slices of bread that he had pinched from the hostel. They sat smoking in the warm sunshine while the supervisor read *The Sun*.

When the supervisor had finished reading the paper, Barry picked it up. The front page was ranting as usual about 'scroungers and dossers' bleeding the country dry.

'Phew, What a Scrounger' was the headline over the story of a 'porn star stunner' who had claimed benefit while filming in the Caribbean. The paper reminded readers that it was their patriotic duty to ring the National Benefit Fraud Hotline if they suspected someone was claiming benefit while working.

Barry threw the paper down in disgust. This was what Gaz used to call benefit porn.

'What's wrong?' asked the supervisor.

'It's bollocks. That's what,' said Barry.

'How do you mean?' asked one of the other lads.

'Well, I don't know about you,' said Barry, 'but I'm not a scrounger. I want to work. Just because I'm claiming benefit it doesn't make me a scrounger. A scrounger in my book is someone who wants something for nothing, right?'

The lad nodded.

'Well, who's getting something for nothing here? The council. Not us. This is unpaid work, isn't it? And we've got no choice, have we? At least in prison they pay you eighty pence a day if you can get a job. How is this not slavery?'

'That's all very well,' said the supervisor, 'but you also have a debt to pay to society.'

'Don't get me wrong,' said Barry. 'I'm happy to tidy up this cemetery. For one thing, it beats sitting in the Jobcentre all day applying for jobs that don't exist. But I would rather be paid for doing this. Why can't the council pay us?'

The supervisor sighed with impatience. 'Because of local authority cut-backs.'

'And whose fault is that? It's not the council workers' fault they lost their jobs. And it's certainly not my fault.'

'But the country can't spend what it hasn't got, can it?' said a lad in a beanie.

'Fair point,' said Barry. 'Benefit fraud costs this country about a billion pounds a year. Which sounds like a lot to you and me. It is a lot. But tax fraud in Britain costs *fifteen* billion every year. Think about it. Every time some poor sod claims a quid when they shouldn't, there's a businessman or a banker somewhere pocketing fifteen. And yet newspapers like this keep banging on about people on benefit living in luxury.'

'You don't have to read it if you don't like it,' said the supervisor. 'It's a free country.'

In the afternoon they raked the grass cuttings into large piles. Then they put the grass into canvas sacks. As he collected up the grass from round the graves Barry found himself reading the worn inscriptions on the headstones, especially the children's graves. Some were long and fancy. Others were plain and heart-felt. He tried to imagine the lives of the dead beneath his feet. Each of them had once been loved by someone. Someone would have cried at each of these graves. Barry did not think anyone would ever shed tears at his graveside.

Later, some kids on the way home from school stopped to watch them working. One of them pointed at their high-vis jackets and jeered. Barry turned to say something, but the kids ran away, giggling.

As they were finishing for the day a group of men in suits turned up. One of them introduced himself as the Community Payback Quality Assurance Manager. The others were from the local council. They all seemed pleased with the improvements to the cemetery, especially the councillors, who beamed for the council photographer.

The minibus dropped the four lads off outside the Jobcentre.

As usual, Jackson was waiting for Barry by the railings. So was Little Chris and one of his minders.

'It's a dog's life, eh, Baz?' said Chris.

Barry did not say anything.

'Nice dog you've got here, Baz. Been in the wars a bit, though, hasn't he?'

Jackson looked uneasily up at Little Chris, then back at Barry. Barry still did not say anything. Jackson flinched when Chris bent down to stroke him.

'Look,' said Chris. 'I won't bother asking if you've found a job. There are no jobs, Baz. You know that. They know that. The only person round here who is going to give you a job is me. I don't know why you are being so fussy. Nice job, money in your pocket, all your debts paid off.'

'What about Abi?' asked Barry.

Chris shrugged. 'What about Abi?'

'How is she?' asked Barry. 'Is she all right?'

'That depends, Baz. Depends on you. You've got till the end of the week . . .'

What do you think?

Is Community Payback a good idea, or is it just a way for the council to get free labour?

Who do you think will shed tears at your grave?

What does Chris mean when he says, 'It's a dog's life'?

11

Skipping

———————————

The food bank was based in the Methodist church hall on Cameron Road. Despite the rain, Barry hesitated outside the front door. It was a very long time since he had been inside a church. Inside it was busy, with people drinking cups of tea and chatting. It looked more like a café than a bank. Barry wondered if he had come to the right place.

'Can I help you?'

Barry turned round. It was a young black woman, her hair braided in cornrows.

'I'm – er – I'm looking for— I mean— I thought— Is this the right place?' Barry was aware that he was not making much sense. He showed the young woman the voucher from the Jobcentre.

She smiled. 'If you mean the food bank, this is the right place. I'm Tembi. I'm a volunteer here.' She offered Barry her hand. 'Can I get you a cup of tea?' She indicated a vacant table by the window.

Barry nodded. 'Thanks. Black, no sugar. Please.'

He sat down at the table while she poured two mugs of tea and brought them over. Barry took a sip of the black, unsweetened tea. He smiled. Unlike Barbara at the hostel, she had actually given him tea just how he had asked for it.

'What's so funny?' asked Tembi.

'Oh, nothing,' said Barry. 'It's just that— When you asked— I mean— Oh, never mind.' He realized he was blushing.

Tembi did not seem to have noticed. She was ticking some boxes on the sheet of paper in front of her. 'Is this your first time here?'

Barry nodded.

'Have you been to a food bank before?'

Barry shook his head. 'They're new, aren't they? There weren't any last time— I mean I've been – I've been away . . .'

'No worries,' said Tembi. 'This is just one of four food banks in town. We're open three mornings a week. So when we're shut, the others are open. You can take your vouchers to any of them. As you can see, we are pretty busy here.

In fact some weeks we can't really cope with the demand. All our food is donated, mostly by churches, schools and individuals. We sort out all the donations into parcels. We have to check the stuff, too. A few months ago we found disposable razor blades in a box of tea and some cat litter in a coffee jar.'

Barry was shocked. 'Why would anyone want to do that?'

'You tell me,' said Tembi. 'Because some people are sick. Because every time you turn on the TV there is someone going on about the "undeserving poor". People come to us for all sorts of reasons. Redundancy, an unexpected bill, loan sharks, zero-hours contracts, part-time work, changes to benefits. You name it.' She sipped her tea. 'Do you know how many people used food banks last year?' Barry shook his head. 'A million. There are officially thirteen million people living below the poverty line. Including kids.'

Barry could not decide if this fact made him feel better or worse about his own situation. At least he did not have children to feed.

He asked, 'What do I have to do?'

'Nothing. In exchange for this voucher we give you an emergency parcel of food. Each parcel contains enough food for three days. Usually tinned tomatoes, tinned tuna, tinned fruit, tinned beans, tinned rice pudding.' She smiled. 'I hope you've got a tin-opener!'

'Funny you should say that.' Barry laughed. He started to tell her about Jackson and the tins of dog food, but she interrupted him, putting her hands over her ears.

'Stop,' she laughed. 'I don't want to hear any more. Seriously. You can laugh about it now, Barry. But what if you had been caught? What then? Back inside for the sake of two tins of dog food?'

Barry frowned. 'How do you know I've been inside?'

Tembi looked at him. 'I've been volunteering here for the past two years. I'm not stupid. I don't care what you did. And it's all the same to me if you want to go back inside. But I don't think Jackson would be very pleased. Do you?'

Barry did not know what to say.

'Tell you what,' said Tembi. 'You think about it while I get some more tea.'

She refilled their mugs and brought over two slices of flapjack. She asked, 'Have you heard of the Freegans?'

'The what?'

'The Freegans,' she said. 'You know, skipping. Skip-diving.'

Barry had no idea what she was talking about.

'If you want to feed your dog you should think about it. The Freegans go around the back of supermarkets at night and help themselves to all the unwanted food. And these days the big shops don't prosecute. It looks bad in the papers. But you should see how much they throw away every day. Most of it is still OK to eat. Most of it's not even past its sell-by date,' Tembi explained.

Barry asked, 'So why do they throw it out?'

'Good question. In some other countries it's against the law for supermarkets to throw away unsold food. They have to give it to charities like us.'

'Well,' said Barry, 'why don't they do that in this country?'

She shrugged. 'The British government say they don't believe in setting targets.'

'Bit rich when you consider all the targets they have for reducing benefit.' Barry liked this girl. 'Any chance of another piece of flapjack?'

'Feel free.'

But Barry did not feel free. Not at all. Something in the phrase made him suddenly well up. And then he found himself talking and talking. About himself. About Abi. About his mum leaving when he was little. About his dad's bike crash. About his nan dying of cancer. And about the years he had wasted in prison. He talked about Jackson. About the old lady whose books were going to landfill. And about all the dead beneath the green grass in the cemetery. He talked and talked until there was nothing left to say. He had no idea why he was talking to this stranger. Except that it kept him from crying. And somehow he knew that she was not going to judge him.

Back in the hostel that night Barry noticed that there was a new girl at the window of the house behind the hostel. And there was a man in the room with her.

It was Little Chris.

What do you think?

Why would people put razor blades in donations to a food bank?

Do you think it should be against the law for supermarkets in the UK to throw away unsold food?

Why do you think that Barry is able to talk to Tembi easily?

12

Rubbish

———◆•◆•◆———

'Wotcha, Barry. All right?'

It was Derek, the *Big Issue* seller. Barry had first met him on his last sentence. Derek was a good-natured Cockney with a big mouth, a bad habit and a pile of unsold magazines at his feet. Barry liked him. He knew that they would have shaken hands if they had met inside. But for some reason it was not the same on the Out.

'You got a job yet?' asked Derek.

'No, mate,' said Barry. 'Just spent another day in the Jobcentre. Waste of time, if you ask me. But I have to go every day or they'll sanction me.'

'You want to get a job, mate,' laughed Derek.

'Tell me about it.'

Derek shook his head. 'No get-up-and-go, you young people. No enterprise. Seize the day, Barry, seize the day!'

Barry could never tell if Derek was being sarcastic or not. 'How do you mean?'

'Well, look at me. I'm a self-made man, me. Because I stand here in all weathers, trying to sell the *Big Issue* and freezing my rocks off, I am officially self-employed. I am what you might call a shining example of the enterprise economy. I've got nowhere to sleep, I do all my shopping in a skip, and yesterday I sold eight copies of the magazine. That's a profit of eight quid. Watch out, Richard Branson!'

'I'd buy a copy just to shut you up,' grinned Barry. 'But I've no money. I'm still waiting for my first benefit payment.'

'Still, I shouldn't complain,' continued Derek. 'It's easier than thieving. And it's a lot better than begging. I've tried that. Horrible. The way people look at you when you ask them for spare change. No one in their right mind would choose to beg on the streets. It's degrading and humiliating. And the police are always on your case. Did you know that begging is a criminal offence?'

Barry rolled a couple of tabs and gave one to Derek.

'There are now so many people living rough, they've started putting CCTV cameras on the bin lorries. You know why? To stop people kipping in empty wheelie-bins.'

'Seriously?' asked Barry.

'Seriously,' nodded Derek. 'And what's wrong with taking a quiet nap in a wheelie-bin? I'll tell you what. Because last year four people were crushed to death when the bins were emptied. Treat people like rubbish and they end up like rubbish.'

Barry frowned. Jackson barked.

'Who's your friend, then?' said Derek.

'You mean Jackson?'

'Jackson? You've named your dog after a dodgy pop singer with a false nose?' laughed Derek.

Barry shook his head. 'Not Michael Jackson, you idiot. George Jackson. And he's not my dog. He just keeps me company. Don't you, boy?' Jackson barked. 'Of course they won't let him in the bail hostel. That reminds me. You know the big house behind the hostel?'

'The house with the lions on the gate? Why?' asked Derek. 'What's it got to do with you?'

'Nothing really. It's just that I saw Little Chris there the other night.'

'You want to stay well clear of the place, Barry,' replied Derek. 'It's a high-class knocking-shop.

A meat-market. Run by some gang. They traffic the girls from all over. Expensive, too, from what I hear. Way above your pay grade.'

Barry suddenly remembered the faces of the girls at the window. Like birds in a cage. He remembered their blank and sad expressions. He felt ashamed to know how wrong he had been about their lives. To think that he had actually envied them . . .

'But isn't it a bit obvious?' he said. 'I mean, it's a residential area, not your usual industrial estate car park.'

'Hidden in plain view, Barry,' said Derek. 'Big house in a residential area. No one notices anything. All the customers are very respectable. Businessmen and councillors with big cars and nice suits.'

'But what's Little Chris got to do with it?'

Derek looked round, as though Little Chris might be listening to their conversation.

'Look, mate,' said Derek, 'if I were you I would forget about the place. The people running it are bad people. I mean *seriously* bad. I have no idea why Little Chris and his firm are involved, but they're a bunch of Teletubbies compared to this lot. Anyway, from what I hear, the place is protected.'

'Protected?' Barry asked.

'Proper protected,' repeated Derek. 'Never mind Jimmy Savile. Remember Rotherham and Rochdale? All those young girls groomed for sex? Or that big hotel in London where politicians and policemen used to hold "kiddies' parties"? Well, this place is like that. There's powerful people involved, Barry. Powerful people.'

Barry suddenly felt sick. To think that all this was going on just behind the bail hostel. How could he not have noticed?

'Apparently it's a kind of holding centre,' Derek continued. 'Import and export, you might say. Girls go one way, drugs go the other. And the money goes straight to the launderette. The girls stay there for a few days, then they're shipped out, especially the under-age ones.'

'Under-age?' asked Barry, although he thought he already knew the answer.

Derek gave a sigh. 'With these people the price goes up as the age goes down. That's market forces. Remember, you can't buck the market, as Mrs Thatcher used to say.'

What do you think?

Why do men shake hands more inside than on the Out?

Why does Derek describe himself as an example of the enterprise economy?

Is it right that begging is a criminal offence?

13

Perfect day

The following Sunday morning, Barry and Jackson were walking on the moors above the town. The sky was a milky pale blue. The clouds on the distant hills were perfect, like the ones you see in *The Simpsons.*

For the first time since getting out, Barry felt free. Really free. Judging by the way that Jackson was running across the heather, chasing rabbits, the dog was also enjoying the freedom of the open air. Better than running round a track making someone money, thought Barry. As someone once said, 'The best things in life are free.'

Freedom. Whatever that meant. The warm wind was in his face and the troubles of the previous week were left behind. Up here there were no forms to fill in, no CCTV cameras, and no one telling him what he could and could not do. He did not need a bank account to enjoy the bright morning sunshine.

He knew that all his immediate problems would be sorted if he agreed to work for Little Chris. But he also knew that if he did, his real problems would just be starting. Even after two years of being clean, Barry was not keen on the idea of being around people selling class A drugs. Not a good idea. And he did not like the sound of Little Chris's new business associates. But since he could not pay back the £800, he had no choice. Unless he disappeared. But that would put him in breach of his licence conditions.

Barry thought about Gaz, still banged up while he was here in the warm sunshine, watching the birds fly high in the sky. Gaz never told Barry what to do, but he had often helped him to think through a difficult decision. Barry sat down in the shade of a stone wall and rolled a tab. Jackson put his head on Barry's knee.

'Looks like you will have to do instead,' said Barry. 'What do you reckon? What would you do?'

Jackson looked up at Barry as though he was thinking about the question.

'I mean, what's the most important thing here – staying out of trouble, or helping Abi?'

Jackson barked.

'What's that supposed to mean?' asked Barry.

Jackson barked again.

'OK. One bark means I work for Little Chris. Two barks mean I don't. Think about it.'

Jackson stared at Barry again, and then barked three times.

On their way home they passed a woman and two small children playing with a kite. They were having difficulty keeping the kite in the air. Suddenly it swooped towards Barry and fell to the ground, almost hitting him. Jackson ran around barking with excitement. The young woman came over with the children to apologize.

'It's OK,' said Barry, picking up the kite. 'It missed.' Then he realized who it was. The girl from the food bank.

'Oh, hi. It's Tembi, isn't it?' asked Barry. As if he didn't know. 'We met at the food bank last week.'

'I remember. Barry the flapjack fan,' she said.

They both laughed.

'Are these—? I mean . . .'

'They're my sister's children, if that's what you mean,' said Tembi. 'Kelly and Marcus. It's Kelly's birthday. We're trying to fly her new kite. Not very successfully, as you can see.'

'It's the lines,' said Barry, untangling the kite's strings. 'They're too tight.' He loosened them and gave the kite back to Tembi. 'Now hold tight and I'll run with the spool.' He ran twenty paces and Tembi let go of the kite. The kite shot straight up into the air, its multi-coloured tail dancing across the wide blue sky.

'Yes!' shouted Tembi. The kids clapped their hands with delight. Jackson ran around barking.

Barry passed the strings to Tembi and sparked up. He watched her while Jackson and the kids ran around after the kite. He liked this girl. So did Jackson.

Eventually the kids tired themselves out. Even Jackson seemed to have had enough. Barry gave Marcus and Kelly piggyback rides on the way back to town. They stopped at a garage and Tembi bought everyone an ice-cream, including Jackson. They sat at the bus stop, eating in silence.

'Nice kids,' said Barry.

Tembi nodded. 'They've taken a real shine to Jackson. And to you,' she added with a smile.

Barry was still trying to decide how to answer this when the bus arrived. Tembi and the kids got on. He waved as the bus pulled away. They waved back. Jackson barked.

Back in the hostel, Barry went straight to his room. He was knackered. He stood at the window, wishing that he had some burn. The words of the old Lou Reed song, 'Perfect Day', were running round his head. Maybe on a day like today he really could forget himself and his problems. He knew that some people said it was a song about heroin. But that was not the reason it was playing in his head tonight. It *had* been just a perfect day.

After a while the light went on in the room of the big house opposite. There was a new girl there. There was a man in the room too. As she stood up to draw the curtains, her long black hair fell away from her face.

It was Abi.

What do you think?

Do you think it is true to say that the best things in life are free?

What does 'freedom' mean to you?

What is your idea of a perfect day?

14

If only

———•◆•———

Barry stared across into the dark space between the houses. Although it was not cold, he could not stop shivering. At the same time he was numb with shock and sick with helpless anger. He tried not to think of the men touching Abi, treating her like a piece of expensive meat, passing her between them as if she was a slave.

The stars were out in force, cold and sharp against the night sky. The moon seemed to be staring at him, challenging him to do something. This was his fault. His fault. His fault. If only he had not been such an idiot. If only he had not spent so long inside. If only he had been better, braver, wiser. If only he could have been the big brother that Abi deserved.

If only, if only. It sometimes felt to Barry that his life was defined by these two words. If only their mum had not left them. If only their dad had not died in the accident. If only Nan had not died of cancer.

But Barry was not in the mood to share the blame. He knew that everything was his fault. His life suddenly seemed like a photo album of shameful memories. His nan collecting him from the police station. The time she caught him stealing the rent money from the tea-caddy in the kitchen. The police searching his nan's bedroom. The Christmas Abi found the track-marks on his arm. The night Dean, one of his best mates, had overdosed. Abi's face in court the last time he was sentenced. The things she had said to him when he got out. There was no place for him to hide.

He looked at the photo of him and Abi that stood next to his bed. The two of them were hanging on a climbing frame, pulling faces like chimps. When he was nine, Nan had taken them on a coach trip to the zoo. Abi must have been about six. Nan had sat smoking on a bench while he took Abi round the monkey-house. Abi had laughed at the monkeys, especially the little ones with cheeky faces.

But there was also something sad in the expressions of some of the bigger monkeys. It was as though they knew that they were locked up for life. He remembered a huge orange orang-utan peering at them through the bars.

Abi had waved. Then the orang-utan threw a stick at them and made Abi cry. A big cage is still a cage, thought Barry. A zoo is like a huge prison. Or maybe prisons are like zoos, full of sad creatures throwing sticks at the bars. As Gaz used to say, 'We are born free, but everywhere people are in chains. The system wants us to polish our chains, not break them.'

There had to be some justice somewhere. Barry thought about the blood-soaked ending of *Taxi Driver*, where Robert de Niro goes banging into the brothel and shoots the pimps and their customers. Even the most patient men snapped one day. 'Suck on this . . .' *Bang!* Barry felt that he knew how Travis Bickle ended up in that bloody hallway, surrounded by all those dead bodies. 'Suck on this . . .' *Bang!* You put up with so much and asked for so little. You did what they told you. You kept your head down. Stayed clean. Tried to find a job. And you never argued back. Not once. Then one day – 'Suck on this . . .' *Bang!*

Barry knew what he had to do. As he got to his feet the last lines of the Lou Reed song were still running round and round his head. 'You're going to reap just what you sow . . .'

What do you think?

Would you agree that it is all Barry's fault?

How are zoos like prisons, and how are they different?

What do you think Barry will do next?

15

Mission impossible

————•◦•————

This takes me back, thought Barry, as he moved quietly down the stairs in the darkness, treading at the edge of each step so that the floorboards did not creak. A radio was playing faintly somewhere on the floor below. The only other sounds were snores and grunts coming from the rooms along the corridor.

As the moon slipped out from behind the clouds, the stairs were suddenly lit with pale moonlight. Barry waited in the shadows for the clouds to return. It was well past curfew. The front door would be locked. The ground-floor windows were either barred or shuttered.

From the first-floor landing he could see the half-open door of the office. There was a bank of CCTV monitors on the office wall. Barry could smell the remains of a Chinese take-away. The duty officer was sitting at the desk with his back to the door.

He was watching a film on his laptop. Judging by the music, it was the latest *Mission Impossible.*

As Tom Cruise jumped off the roof of a burning building, Barry crept down the last few stairs. The last step groaned under his foot. Barry froze. The duty officer did not move from his seat.

There was a cupboard under the stairs where cleaning things were kept. Barry almost fell over a mop and bucket as he squeezed into the cupboard and closed the door behind him. He left just enough of a gap so he could watch the office.

He knew that if he was caught he would be shipped straight back to prison. But it was a risk he had to take, for Abi's sake. From what Derek had said, there was no point going to the police. If the place was really 'protected', it would only put Abi in more danger.

Barry wished that he could talk to someone about what he was about to do. What would Gaz say? Or Tembi? But there was no time now to discuss his options. He had to do something straight away, before Abi was sold on. Once she had left the big house he would never be able to find her.

On the laptop Tom Cruise was still doing his stuff. But it was not enough to keep the duty officer awake. The snoring was almost as loud as the soundtrack. Barry slowly opened the door of the cupboard and moved through the shadows towards the office, staying out of the view of the camera by the front door.

The duty officer was still asleep, his mouth hanging open like a frog catching flies. Barry looked round the office. Then he saw what he wanted, sticking out of the top pocket of a jacket on the back of a chair. Barry crawled round the desk until he reached the chair. The duty officer carried on snoring. Barry slipped his hand into the jacket pocket. As he did so, the duty officer gave a sudden start, noisily choking and grunting in his sleep. Barry held his breath. The snoring began again.

Back in his room, Barry sat and looked at the mobile. He could not quite believe he was about to do this. His plan might not work. If it did not, things could be a lot worse for him and for Abi. He just had to hope it would.

He took a deep breath and keyed in the number. After three rings the phone was picked up and a recorded voice said, 'You have reached the National Benefit Fraud Hotline . . .'

What do you think?

What would Gaz and Tembi say to Barry if
   they could see him hiding in the cupboard?

Why do you think Barry is ringing the
   National Benefit Fraud Hotline?

Do you think that Barry is a grass?

16

Payback time

———•◦•———

Abi was asleep. The young policewoman had told Barry he could sit with Abi for five minutes, on the condition that he did not wake her. He sat on the edge of the chair by the bed and watched his sister as she slept.

Abi had lost weight since he last saw her. Her face was thinner. Her eyes were darker. But she was still his beautiful kid sister. Her raven-black hair was spread across the pillow. She looked so young. It was impossible to imagine what she had been through. He hoped that her dreams were as peaceful as the look on her face.

It was all over the front page of the local paper:

Following an anonymous tip-off, Department of Work and Pensions staff investigating benefit fraud were called to a house on Lynnefield Avenue in the early hours of Thursday morning. On entering the house they found evidence of what the police are calling a major international sex-trafficking operation.

A substantial amount of money and quantities of class A drugs have been recovered from the property. Nine young women discovered on the premises have been taken into police protection, and are now receiving medical attention. Five men, including two foreign nationals, have been charged under the Sexual Offences Act (2003) and are currently helping the police with their enquiries . . .

Little Chris had been one of the men arrested. He would not be bothering Barry or Abi for a while. He put the paper down on the bed. The white starched sheets were like a blank page, he thought. Or a new leaf. Maybe this really was a new start for him and Abi.

He would have to give it time, of course. So much had happened between them and so little had ever been said. And there was so much he wanted to say to Abi. He would have to introduce her to Jackson. Maybe even to Tembi.

He left the photo of him and Abi at the zoo on the table by the bed. She would see it when she woke up. He hoped it would make her smile. At least she would know that he had been to see her. Then he let himself out. He would be back first thing tomorrow. Sod the Jobcentre. Some things in life are more important than money.

What do you think?

Do you think it is likely that Barry and Tembi will get together?

How realistic is Barry being about his future relationship with Abi?

What do you think is more important than money?

17

In your dreams

Barbara was waiting for him when he got back to the hostel. 'Must be your birthday, Barry!' she beamed, handing him a pile of letters. Barry frowned. In his experience, letters almost always brought bad news. He took the letters outside and rolled a tab.

The first was from Gaz, full of news from inside – who was back in, who was on Seg, who had been shipped out. Houseblock 3 had won this month's five-a-side competition. There had been a suicide on the 2s. Not long ago this had been Barry's entire world. But now it all seemed very distant. Gaz and the other lads still inside seemed somehow frozen in time. Barry suddenly realized how much he had grown up in the past few weeks.

The second letter was from the benefit office. His claim for Universal Credit had been turned down. Barry was under investigation for claiming benefit while working.

Someone must have seen him helping Craig empty the old lady's house. If he wanted to avoid being recalled he would have to convince them he was just helping out an old friend.

The third letter was from probation. He rolled another tab before he opened it. The letter informed Barry that he was required to attend a new course in order to discuss his hopes and dreams. Barry did not know whether to laugh or cry. Dreams were dangerous things, expensive and full of painful disappointment.

All Barry wanted was an ordinary life. A useful job and a decent flat. Abi safe and well. Probation off his back. And then there was Tembi . . .

It wasn't a lot to ask. Was it?

What do you think?

Why does Barry think that dreams are expensive?

In what ways does this feel like a happy ending?

What are your dreams for the future?

FEEDBACK FORM

cliffusion

We hope you enjoyed *Bare Freedom*. Please help us by filling in this short form. By telling us a bit about yourself, you will help us to make our books better in the future.

(1) What is the name of your prison?

Thank you for your feedback. Please send this feedback form back to us and we will try to send you another book in the series.

(2) Are you:

☐ a prisoner
☐ a group facilitator
☐ a librarian
☐ a prison officer
☐ a chaplain
☐ other (please state)

PLEASE RETURN THIS FEEDBACK FORM TO:
PRISON FICTION PROGRAMME
SPCK
36 CAUSTON STREET
LONDON
SW1P 4ST

(3) Did you like the book?

☐ Yes   ☐ No

(4) Did you find the book helpful?

☐ Yes   ☐ No

(5) Can you tell us why?